# Bouncing Back from Failure

Also by Adom Appiah

Kids Can Change the World

A middle schooler's guide for turning passion into progress

# BOUNCING BACK FROM FAILURE

## ADOM APPIAH

Triple A Press

## Dedication

This book is dedicated to my Spartanburg Day School family. Thank you for teaching me to stand out.

# Acknowledgments

The truth is I couldn't have written this book if I hadn't failed or been disappointed a few times. I'm thankful for my wins and losses! Massive thanks to my Spartanburg Day teachers for keeping me straight. I wrote this book because I wanted to inspire kids about their future. I believe that we all have different abilities. I'd like to thank my family, and friends for their presence and support. A big thank you to the Spartanburg County Foundation for their partnership. I'd also like to thank the Scripps National Spelling Bee for giving me a platform to share the Ball4Good story. Special thanks to Mr. Billy Webster for giving me the idea to expand beyond basketball. And of course, the biggest thank you to my mom and dad.

# TABLE OF CONTENTS

## **A Note to YOU**

Every success has a journey. There will always be bumps in the road, but with perseverance and positivity, nearly any end goal can be reached. Don't be discouraged when things aren't looking up for you. Open your eyes; greater things lie beyond failure. Trust me, when you're able to bounce back from your losses, the feeling of accomplishment will make the journey worthwhile.

Disappointment is part of life. We can't have everything that we want. Even when we work hard and do our best, there is a chance that we might not succeed.

In my first book- Kids Can Change the World, one of the steps for changing the world was to not Fear

Failure. The truth is that when you fail, it's hard to think about the positives. Nobody likes bad news. I've noticed that just as it's hard for kids to deal with disappointments, adults have a hard time handling negative news too.

Although I am young, I know that disappointments are part of life. There are so many things that can have a negative impact on us. It could range from school work to life at home to even making friends. It's okay if things don't work out, keep doing your best.

Know that there is somebody out there going through the same thing that's happening to you. Find the energy to recharge and start over. You may be surprised at the outcome.

My journey has not been smooth. I've had some bumps in the road. Thankfully, I haven't given up. It takes a lot of work behind the scenes.

I want to share the keys to my success with you. There is no such thing as losing. You either win, or you learn. After reading this book, you'll be ready to go out into the world and chase your victories!

## Disappointment

In 2018, I had the opportunity to go back and
compete in the Scripps National Spelling Bee.
Although I enjoyed the second experience, I did
not do as well as I had wanted. It's hard to forget
the moment when I misspelled. Hearing that
dreaded bell was unreal.

It was the afternoon of the third round. I spent the
morning going over spelling rules and was
confident that I was going to ace my word and
move on to the next level.

The journey had not been easy. For the first time, I
had finished reading the Merriam Webster
dictionary. Although it had been a busy school
year, I always made time to learn my spelling
words. There were times that I carried my

dictionary with me on road trips and to my soccer games.

Everything seemed to point to success. Not only had I spent almost a year preparing for victory, I had been dreaming of that moment since third grade.

As I walked towards the stage to take my seat, I started feeling the nervousness in my legs. And as always, I started praying in my head. I was reciting Isaiah 41:10 silently.

When the spelling round started, my confidence crept back. I was spelling all the words right. Before long, it was my turn. I walked up to the microphone. I took a moment to soak in the experience. And then, I smiled at the audience.

The pronouncer mentioned my word. The tension in my legs kicked up a notch. 'Frustraneous' - I knew the word. But I was going to stall a little bit. I asked for the definition, the language of origin and all the possible questions I could ask before spelling. Let's go. I thought in my head.

I began to spell – exuding the confidence that one feels when they prepare well for a task. Out of nowhere, like a faraway dream, I heard the dreaded bell. My stomach flipped! This couldn't be over! I was crushed. I had dreamed of making the final that night.

As I walked towards the 'cookie couch' to meet my parents, I felt the disappointment in my chest. It really hurt. I was disappointed in myself. Dad walked up to me and gave me a hug. I looked for mom but she was nowhere to be found. I felt very sad. I thought I had disappointed her. All the countless coaching hours. I didn't realize that she was with my friend Caleb – who was also upset.

When dad and I walked out of the room, I saw mom. From a distance, I saw her smile. Then I heard her screaming across – 'that's my boy.' She was elated when she saw me. She couldn't stop telling me how proud she was. Right behind mom was my teacher Ms. Cobourn - also with a reassuring smile. Ms. Cobourn had travelled to DC to support me. All 3 adults were proud of how far I'd come. The hugs were priceless.

It didn't take too long to realize that some of my speller friends were quite upset. So, I decided that I was going to make the best out of my situation by encouraging the friends who had misspelled. Little did I know that other people were observing my actions.

A reporter came up to talk to me about my experience. A college recruiter gave me his business card. My reaction to the defeat had turned into something positive. It was a good feeling. Going to Ben & Jerry's for ice cream made it even better. Spartanburg Day School paid for our ice cream!

For a moment, I thought I was okay with my loss. But then, when I got back to the hotel room, the sadness came back. I couldn't believe that my spelling career was over. I felt the disappointment in my stomach.

Even long after my family went to bed, I lay in the sofa bed, mulling about my day. Wishing that I could turn back the time. I wished I could go back on stage and rewrite history. I went to bed knowing that I was never going to get the opportunity to spell on stage as a finalist because I had aged out of the program.

My dreams were dashed and it was okay to be sad rather than pretend that it never happened. I thought about all the years of practice. Not only was I disappointed in my performance, but I also thought about everyone who had faith in me.

We had spent a lot of time, money and energy on preparing for the bee. People had tuned in from all over the world – from my home state of South Carolina to my family's global network.

9

I especially thought about my granddaddy, who had helped me decipher my Latin roots. When I was feeling down during the earlier spelling round, it was granddaddy who cheered me up over the phone. Eventually, I drifted off to a restless sleep.

When I woke up the next morning, my first thought was that maybe it was a dream. I lay in the bed upset. I thought to myself, what am I going to do next? Spelling had been such an integral part of our everyday lives and I hadn't really thought about high school or life after spelling.

My experience taught me that you can still fail at a task even when you prepare. Also, I accepted that praying about something didn't mean that things will go my way. God's plan may be different from mine.

Dad says there's a reason for everything. That couldn't be truer. My DC experience was one of the greatest inspirations that led to me writing this book.

Discovering the reasons for your successes and failures can be an eye-opening process that leads to positive results. For example, writing about my spelling experience is therapeutic.

As the adults say, experience is the best teacher. If you always succeed at stuff, you may become complacent. As I head into high school, I know it's not going to be easy. Yet, the doses of failure that I have encountered along my elementary and middle school experience has prepared me for the journey that lies ahead.

Don't be discouraged when things don't go your way. Set a standard for yourself. Somebody is always going to be better than you. Just form your personal list of do's and don'ts. That way, the next time you put your mind to something, you can trust your own formula to success. You can do it. We just have to keep doing our best and maybe one day our best will be good or even better.

## Adomski's Keys

Are you ready to bounce back after your disappointment? There are a few strategies that have helped me in the past. I call them Adomski's keys to success.

**The Keys:**

1. Work Hard
2. Stay Motivated
3. Maintain a Positive Attitude
4. Communicate Effectively
5. Take Responsibility for your Actions
6. Feel the Emotion
7. Take Chances
8. Have a Good Plan
9. Create a Support System
10. Let's Go!

## Key 1

## Hard Work Pays Off

Every story starts somewhere. Even your favorite professional athletes weren't always at the top of their game. As many know, Michael Jordan was cut from his high school basketball team. However, with perseverance and hard work, he proved his doubters wrong.

Sometimes it's hard to persevere. I spent several games sitting on the bench during basketball. I really wanted to play but I needed to work on my game. After years of practice, I finally started making some good plays.

The hard work paid off in 2017 when I started playing for Coach Gray. Coach gave me the opportunity to start for my team. Because Coach believes in me, I am motivated to practice my jump shots more often. I'm not the star player on my team, but with perseverance, I'm improving my skills.

If you are a football fan, you're probably familiar with the New England Patriots and their winning streak. Their 2018 quarterback is Tom Brady. Brady is now a legend. However, most people don't know that he was drafted in the sixth round of the 2000 NFL draft. He was the 199th overall pick. When Brady started with his team, he was the fourth-string quarterback. He took over as quarterback in his second season after the main quarterback got injured.

Over the years, Brady has guided his team to numerous wins. As of 2018, he'd won the Super Bowl 5 times. Through all the ups and downs of his career, Tom Brady has persevered. He continues to work hard every season.

Sometimes all we see is the end-product of hard work. We may not realize that the person put a lot of effort into their work. My friend Zion Williamson is one example of a hard worker.

When Zion was 5 years old, he had a vision to play basketball. As he got older, he realized that he would like to go to Duke and play for Coach K. Every morning, Zion woke up at 5 am to practice before going to school. There were some mornings when he was the one who woke his stepfather up for practice.

Throughout the years, he practiced his craft and kept improving. By the time he was in 11th grade, he had received several offers to play college basketball. During his senior year, he was named the number 2 player in the country. He received several national and state awards. In the fall of 2018, Zion will be attending his dream college, Duke University.

Having watched Zion play, I can say without a doubt that he is talented. There have been times when Zion had to sit on the bench because of injury. However, he never gives up and is constantly working to improve his skills.

Another example of a hard worker is basketball star Steph Curry. Curry was not a number one pick. He worked and trained hard to become a great NBA player. When you watch Curry's Intense Workout training videos on YouTube, you will be reminded that if you want to excel, you must do the work.

You can't just sit there and think that you are going to get the best grades or be the best athlete. You have to work hard to improve your chances. There are a few people who are super talented and don't have to try hard. But most of us, don't fall into that category.

My spelling friends spend a lot of time battling the dictionary. During the finals at the Bee, I was amazed at the skill level of the spellers. Spelling is like a sport. When you do the work, you get to go on stage and spell!

## Bouncing Back from Failure

One of my mantras in life is to work hard and inspire many. My wish is for everybody to find some kind of success in their life.

In everything that we do, it pays off to persevere. There have been times that I have struggled with some subjects at school, but I try not to give up. I look for ways to make things better. It doesn't always get better.

I had to opt out of art because I could not improve my art skills and grades. One time, I signed up for baseball. That didn't go too well. I just kept messing up. I persevered through the heat, but by the time camp ended, I knew baseball was not for me.

We cannot be good at everything. Everybody has a talent. So, if you discover your talent or identify a passion, work hard at it. You may not succeed the first few times, but keep trying, you may become an expert!

My friend Nana Addo once said that "dedication separates the best from the rest!"

## Key 2

## Stay Motivated

It's hard to stay motivated when things don't go your way. In the spring of 2018, our soccer team traveled to Hilton Head to play in the State semifinals. On our way to Hilton Head, our bus broke down.

Although we arrived at the game on time, we were tired by the time we arrived. Within the first few minutes of starting the game, the opposing team scored. Within 20 minutes, they had scored a few more goals. This made it hard for our team to come back.

Eventually, we lost the game. We were sad. However, our coach encouraged us about our potential. He told us he was very proud of how far we'd come. Although we lost the game, we are determined to come back stronger next soccer season.

There can be different sources of motivation in your life.

I learned a great deal from my time at the 2018 Scripps National Spelling Bee. This year's winner, Karthik Nemmani, lost his county bee to the girl who was $2^{nd}$ place at Nationals this year. Can you believe that? He could have been crushed due to his loss. Instead, he monitored the bee and realized that his opening was through a program called RSVBee. Once he applied and began studying, the rest was history. Karthik's story is legendary, as he was the winner of the largest bee as of 2018. It's just yet another example of the power of staying motivated.

Sometimes it is easy to lose interest. Especially when things are not going your way. $8^{th}$ grade band was tough for me at the beginning of the school year. I was focused on other things and kind of put band on the back burner. I forgot about my class project and didn't even check in with my teacher, Mr. Barnes.

Mr. Barnes was not going to cut me any slack. He gave me a zero on the project. This was a wakeup call. I knew I had to pick up my pace if I was going to get a good band grade. The motivation to make up for my grade kept me going. I paid more attention to my work and ended up with an A at the end of the school year. It was hard making up for that zero but I focused on the end result and the big picture.

If you keep the right mindset, your success story is in the making. Believe me, chasing your dreams isn't as daunting of a task as it seems. Stay motivated and work hard towards your goals.

## Key 3

## Positive Attitude

It's hard to have a positive attitude all the time. When I decided to write this book, I came up with a plan. I will write for 2 hours every morning during the summer. This way, I will have the rest of the day to myself to play or just hang out.

My plan was not realistic. The writing process has been difficult. Most of the time, I don't feel like writing or doing any work. It's been hard to stick to a schedule.

Developing a positive attitude towards writing has helped me a lot. By being proactive, it's been easier to put my thoughts on paper. Attitude can make or break a project.

For example, during sports, I realize that our team spirit affects our performance. In my experience, a positive attitude increases our chance of success and helps us see the possibilities.

For situations where there isn't a next time, there is more difficulty balancing your thoughts. If you are one to put pressure on yourself (like me), then you may feel a blend of anger and disappointment when things don't go your way.

It'll be natural to pick out all your mistakes without appreciating how far you've come. Of course, it is human nature to want more than what you have. Trust me, even when you succeed, you'll still look at what could've been better. This is why it is ALWAYS important to focus on positive thoughts and words.

I'd like to share some advice that I received from my mentor Ms. Mary Thomas.

One time, I was upset during a Ball4Good meeting because I really wanted to be at soccer practice. My bad attitude showed. And the meeting was not productive. I was lucky to have Ms. Thomas advise me on how to put my best foot forward at all times.

She told me to think and act like a CEO and to keep committee members engaged in the process. Ms. Thomas' advice helped me to remember to be confident, grateful and to believe in myself. I'm very lucky to have a mentor who wants to invest in me.

Ms. Thomas' advice paid off. Changing my attitude at the Ball4Good meetings helped our team to collaborate more effectively.

Often, when I observe my surroundings, I notice that my friends who have good attitudes find it easier to talk to more people. This strategy is a good icebreaker.

For example, getting into new activities can be a nerve-wracking process. Let's say you're joining a new sports team. No matter how confident you are in your ability, you'll probably have some nerves at the back of your mind. People may judge your entire ability on the first impression you make.

The best thing you can do in a situation like this is stay positive. With that positive energy, you'll attract the best players to be your friends. Even if you aren't as good as them, try to make a joke or two to lighten the mood. With your positive attitude, you'll eventually feel like part of the team. And when a team is connected, it's easier to win.

Don't forget that it is important to enjoy what you are doing. When you are having fun, harder tasks seem a little easier. Also, time passes faster.

Remember, talent can probably get you a win, but a positive attitude combined with character are the true traits of a champion.

## Key 4

## Communicate

One day, during the past academic school year, I got ready for school. To my knowledge, that day was going to be average. I was looking forward to recess, sports practice, and learning new things.

However, this all changed when I walked into the Science classroom and got my test back. My expression quickly changed to a concerned one. I had earned a dreaded C on the test!

A billion thoughts whirred through my head at that moment. How could I possibly make this better? While we were going over answers, it dawned on me. I was going to have to go out of my comfort zone.

Bouncing Back from Failure

An important part of success is communication. Given that this isn't really one of my skills, I used to do my best to avoid it. Monosyllabic answers were typically my go-to if asked a question. However, my approach was different in this case.

I knew that if my teacher (Mr. Burnham) didn't know what I was thinking, nothing was going to change. After class, I worked up the confidence to ask what I could do about my test. I was met with my teacher's smile and advice. Mr. Burnham told me that I couldn't change that particular grade, but if I wanted guidance, his doors were open.

This experience was a stepping stone for me. Not only did my next grades improve, but my confidence did as well. I was more open to discussing my grades with my teachers and parents. Who would have known that the loss I took that day would actually be for the better? I sure didn't!

The moral of the story is to let you know that effective communication can open doors and help you solve problems. You may not know the answer if you don't ask. Also, communication can help you clarify stuff that you don't understand.

Do not let your failures define you, but rather, let your recoveries be a testament to your character. Despite falling short at the beginning of the school year, Mr. Burnham never gave up on me. He told me what I needed to do to make things right. Thankfully, I got a good grade because of the extra effort and clarification.

If you are having difficulty with your school work or other projects, don't be afraid to talk to your teachers. They may be able to help you understand the problem or provide you with an alternate solution.

## Key 5

## Take Responsibility

When I got my C in science, my first reaction was to place blame. Maybe I was juggling too many activities. Maybe the teacher didn't explain well enough. Both accusations were obviously false. However, in my defeated mind, they made perfect sense.

Sometimes I don't like to take responsibility for my actions. For example, when I forget to turn in my homework, I try to make excuses. Sometimes I blame it on sports or other projects.

However, with help from Mrs. Richardson, my middle school principal, I'm trying to be more responsible for my school work. Mrs. R. has taught me that it's important to own up to your mistakes. I'm really hoping that I'll take the necessary responsibility in high school.

Middle school life taught me that it's important to be prepared for the letdowns. Know that lost opportunities prepare you for the next step.

Instead of dwelling on the mistakes, simply acknowledge them and learn from them. Although it's hard to own up to your mistakes it's better to acknowledge your faults than to make excuses.

A simple way to take responsibility for your actions is to make a pro/con list. See where you performed well as opposed to where you made mistakes. This is always helpful to me because it gives me time to reflect on my journey. Once you pinpoint certain aspects of the situation, it can feel like a weight lifted off your shoulders.

Next, prepare for another opportunity that may come your way. Your next opportunity will be easier to manage because of the lessons you've taught yourself.

## Key 6
## Emotions are Good

It's okay to be sad when you fail. You don't need a scientific study to tell you that messing up is no fun.

Nonetheless, science can help us understand how to respond to our mistakes so we can learn from what happened and win the next time around. Believe it or not, advice like "sucking it up" may not be the best route to go.

A study in the *Journal of Behavioral Decision Making* found that people who allowed themselves a little time to feel self-pity after failing at a task were more successful in the future compared to those who tried to rationalize and move on immediately from what happened.

In the initial test, people were asked to search online for the cheapest blender they could find, with the possibility of winning a $50 cash prize. Unbeknownst to the participants, the experiment was designed for everyone to fail.

After everybody's inevitable failure, researchers asked participants to write down how they felt about losing. Some were instructed to focus on their emotions — and experienced thoughts like, "Ugh, I can't believe I did that," "I don't want to feel like this ever again," and "I didn't do my best." Others were asked to think "cognitively" about their failure, for example, "I wouldn't have won anyway" and "This wasn't important."

For the second experiment, participants were given a budget and asked to peruse the internet for a book to buy a friend while scientists measured how many minutes they spent looking.

"We found that the people who'd focused on their emotional responses spent nearly 25 percent more time searching for a low-priced book than those who only reflected cognitively on their failure," says co-author Selin A. Malkoc, associate professor of marketing at Ohio State University.

It's true that we should rationalize mistakes to a degree. If we didn't we'd go nuts beating ourselves up. However, when we stop to process our emotions, our innate ability to change and be resourceful kicks in.

"Neuroscience studies show that when we feel strongly enough about something, the brain 'tags' it and when a similar situation arises in the future, we draw from that emotion to find solutions," says Malkoc.

Malkoc and her team's discoveries are actually closely related to the workplace or classroom. This is because both are spaces where performance is constantly being assessed by supervisors.

The findings are relevant to everyday life. Just as it's okay to celebrate and be happy when you succeed, it's fine to be sad or upset when you fail.

So next text time you screw up, allow yourself to acknowledge negative feelings. Sit quietly with those emotions for a bit, but not too long.

In my case, I allow myself to feel bad when things don't go my way. However, my mood lasts more than five minutes. Maybe as I get older, I will learn how to manage my emotions better. But what I know is that every failure prepares me for my next opportunity.

## Key 7

## Take a Chance

When it comes to taking on tasks, you have to believe in yourself. You should be your biggest fan. Without self-confidence, nearly all your endeavors will pose as a challenge. Several stories prove the point that belief in oneself creates a pathway for success.

A great example of this is the journey of fashion designer Virgil Abloh. Kanye West noticed Abloh's potential in 2002. Subsequently, Kanye appointed Abloh as his creative consultant. Abloh has been steadily rising ever since.

In 2009, Abloh began working on his first label, Pyrex Vision. His brand blew up due to his celebrity connections. Before he knew it, his brand was on its way to becoming mainstream. Abloh had an even bigger dream. Through Pyrex Vision, he had established himself and laid the ground work for his world-famous brand, Off-White.

Abloh always had a taste in fashion that wasn't necessarily mainstream. Nevertheless, he was confident that others would share his taste. By building his portfolio, he was able to make others see the beauty in odd designs.

For those who don't know, Off-White clothes are often asymmetrical. Some may even look tattered or worn. Normally, it would be difficult to convince *anybody* to wear some of the designs. However, with the clout Abloh had gained, he was ready to be the fashion innovator of our generation.

Today, Virgil Abloh is praised as a creative genius, an icon, and an inspiration to believers everywhere. He has been the director of Louis Vuitton's men's wear collection since March 2018. Abloh is living proof that if you love what you do, the possibilities of your impact are endless.

It takes sacrifice. Sometimes you may not feel like doing the work. It can even get harder because of social media. Can you imagine checking your Instagram feed to find your friends having fun when you are stuck behind a project? Not fun! If it's that hard for you, maybe you should delete some of your apps. I read somewhere that there've been times that LeBron has stayed off social media during the NBA playoffs.

Mind you, I'm not saying that you should constantly be working on your craft. If it works for you to stay focused 24/7, why not, go ahead. However, if you are like me then you might need a little break here and there. What matters is that you maintain a healthy balance. This way, you are neither too stressed nor too relaxed.

It pays to believe and take a chance on yourself. Brazil may not have won the 1958 World Cup if 17-year-old Pelé hadn't taken the chance to display his Ginga style of play.

## Key 8

## Plan!

Having a plan is important. It's good to be prepared for every situation. You are either going to win or lose. But if you don't start, you won't know the outcome.

When I was younger, I thought that it was easy to become a doctor because most of the people that I met were doctors. As I got older, I thought that the professionals in my family were very smart. I began to learn the truth when I was 11 years old.

One of my aunts got accepted into medical school so we went to her white coat ceremony. Each student had to choose a word to describe their journey. My aunt's word was 'perseverance'. That day, I learned about my aunt's road to medical school. She had worked very hard by writing several exams and by crafting a plan for her medical school applications.

Soon after, I learned about how my Uncle P got accepted to the University of Virginia. Although Uncle P is an American, he immigrated from Ghana when he won the green card lottery. The first time he applied for college, he was not accepted into the schools that he wanted.

He didn't give up. He enrolled in college and tried again when he was ready for grad school. Now, he's an engineer with a really cool job!

Before long, I learned about the difficulties my dad faced before getting into a medical residency program. Dad worked unpaid jobs until he finally matched to start working at a hospital.

As I listened to the adults' stories about their struggles, I realized that it was key for me to try my best at all times.

I'd like to tell you about my Plan A to C story.

My Plan A was to win the school bee and represent my school at Regionals. I had envisioned the win since the summer of $3^{rd}$ grade.

After winning my $3^{rd}$ grade class bee, Mrs. Sonia LeCroy advised me to watch the Scripps National Spelling Bee on TV.

The year was 2013. That was the year that Arvind Mahankali won. I was encouraged to see a boy take the top prize in the bee. I made a promise to myself that one day, I was going to spell on the national stage.

In 2016, I was a 6$^{th}$ grader with big dreams to win the bee. I remember picking up the spelling folder from Ms. Cobourn and practicing every day. At one point, I emailed her to ask about what happened when we finish the words in the folder. Ms. Cobourn quickly replied by telling me that, that never happens at our school. This was good news! I was confident that I could spell all the words in that yellow folder.

The afternoon of the bee, we made history at SDS. We finished all the words in the folder so Ms.

Cobourn and her team had to introduce the next set of words. There were two of us left standing. It was me and the $8^{th}$ grade reigning champion, Ellie Toler.

As the rounds progressed, I missed my word and Ellie was declared the winner. Plan A to represent my school had fallen through. It was time to focus on Plan B - my dream to participate in a math competition for my school.

In $6^{th}$ grade, I was bumped up to the Pre-Algebra $7^{th}$ class. This was exciting because I had been looking forward to participating in Mathcounts since $4^{th}$ grade. I was certain that if I was good enough to be in Pre-Algebra then I will be chosen for the team.

To make the team, Ms. V gave us a test. I was confident about my performance. However, when the results came, I made the practice squad as an alternate. It was good news. I was able to practice with the squad, but I was still disappointed.

Plan B hadn't gone as planned. However, plan C was in the works.

I was determined to represent my school in an academic competition. I knew that I was an alternate speller for regionals so I was already mastering the words on Spellit (a spelling resource).

Luckily for me, Ellie had a conflict and couldn't go to regionals. She offered me the opportunity to represent our school.

Plan C was underway. The good thing is that I had already started preparing.

I didn't know how my trip to regionals was going to turn out. Nobody had ever made finals from our school. My goal was to be one of the finalists. I wanted to go to the bee, check out how it was done and go prepare for nationals the following year.

Well, the hard work paid off. Plan C worked. I made it to the finals stage during regionals and even placed third! I don't think I'd ever been that happy to be third place!

So, you see, having alternate plans worked for me. The goal was to represent my school in an academic competition. And with a lot of hard work, it happened.

My family's story of academic perseverance inspires me to try my hardest. It's not always easy, but I'm determined to overcome the obstacles in my way.

My experience so far has shown me that it's good to have a plan and to set goals. You may not always achieve your goals but when you have a plan, it's easier to bounce back.

People think that our generation is lazy, play video games and live our lives on social media. Let's show them that we've got goals and that we can make it happen! Let's not give up when things don't go our way. We can always find ways to turn things around. Let's learn from our experiences and plan for tomorrow.

## Key 9

## Your Support System

"If you want to go fast in life, go alone. If you want to go far, work together." – My Nana.

We all need someone on our journey. Your person could be an adult, a friend or a family member.

For example, when I started playing Fortnite (a video game), it was hard for me to advance. I just had to play for 30 seconds before dying in the game. Although I kept trying, I just couldn't master the skill. Luckily for me, my friends came to the rescue. We played as a squad and they helped me get better.

It's helpful to have a support system. However, be careful with the people that you affiliate yourself with. Some people may not have your best interest at heart. One time, I received an email from an author who offered to help me promote my first book. He asked me to call him. Luckily, I shared the information with my mom. When we called, we realized that he was a fraud.

As I think back about my Ball4Good journey, I realize that Ball4Good's success is a result of several collaborations. I've had a lot of help from my family, friends, mentors, teachers, organizations and my community. The support that I've received has helped me make better decisions.

For example, during the planning phase of the second celebrity games, I realized that my fundraising strategy was falling short. I was almost certain that we would not reach our fundraising goal. Then Mrs. Booker – a member of the planning committee came to the rescue.

Through a brainstorming session, she suggested that we encourage our teams to compete against each other on the fundraising platform. Thanks to Mrs. Booker's idea, the players helped Ball4Good to exceed the fundraising goal.

Success is often a result of positive peer pressure. When you surround yourself with go-getters, you'll find yourself wanting to be great. However, if you are surrounded by lazy people, your productivity won't be too impressive.

The importance of a support system became even clearer to me after the 2018 spelling bee experience.

Throughout bee week, I observed my fellow spellers who performed exceptionally well. I noticed that they were all friends. They cheered each other on.

I learned from these friends and was motivated to help others experience the fun in reading and spelling.

Shortly after bee week, I ran an idea by my speller friends, and we've started a new initiative called RiseToBee. We want to be able to provide more spellers with the opportunity to achieve their goals.

The best part about this is that we are all excited to help. With our strong team of smart, hard workers, we are ready to make a difference.

However, since we started the RiseToBee program, we have hit some roadblocks. We now know that it's going to be hard to raise $6,000 every year to sponsor a kid from a region for nationals. Although we've realized that our initial goals were lofty, we are still working as a team to find the best way to impact more spellers.

Having a support system applies to every facet of our lives. However, it's not always easy to have someone to talk to about your strategy.

There may be times when you will feel that other people probably don't get you. Don't be discouraged. You are not alone. I think it happens to a lot of us. Maybe you can read a good book or listen to encouraging music. The kind of music you listen to can help you through some tough times.

Overall, I am grateful for the support that's available on my journey. A LOT of people have helped me come this far. I keep these people around me. They make me want to work hard and to reach my full potential. Although I may not always show it, I don't take anything or anyone for granted.

My wish is that you will also find your support system. With strong support, you can truly dare to dream about your awesome future. Let's surround ourselves with positive role models and friends who will motivate us.

## Key 10

## Let's Go!

Mom says, "he who is down need fear no fall."

You are never at the end of the road. You can always give yourself a pep talk to get back in the game. Sometimes life can be tough, but don't give up.

In the fall of 2016, our history class began working on our 20Time projects. 20Time is a project in which you dedicate 20% of your class time (one day a week) to an endeavor helping something or someone.

When I started working on my project, my initial thought was to teach computer classes at an assisted living facility. Since I had been learning how to code, the idea sounded perfect.

I was excited about our project. However, after we began the process, I realized that I had lost interest.

I found the courage to tell my classmate that I was no longer interested in the project. Next, I had to inform my teacher. Unfortunately for me, I lost all the points from the computer project when I changed my mind.

However, I was determined to get myself back in the game. After bouncing ideas off my family and friends, I settled on doing a project that can impact my community through sports.

The brainstorming finally led to the formation of Ball4Good. Ball4Good is now a nonprofit supporting communities through sports.

With a lot of guidance from my teacher, mentor, friends and community, we organized our first Ball4Good Celebrity Games in March 2017.

Working on Ball4Good hasn't been easy. I've made mistakes along the way. However, I am encouraged to keep working hard towards my goals. My mistakes serve as stepping stones toward greater successes.

Failure prepares us for future opportunities. I believe that we have to keep doing our best at all times.

It's likely that you won't be good at everything. Nevertheless, you can still use your skills and dreams to change the world.

When you mess up, don't beat yourself up. Everybody makes mistakes. Sometimes we pay a big price for our mistakes, but it's part of the learning process. Experience is the best teacher.

When you fail at something, cheer yourself up. You should have the inner belief that everything you're doing is for a future positive outcome. **Don't give up easily. Keep trying. Eventually, success will happen.**

We can rebound from failure. With determination, perseverance and hard work, we can achieve our goals.

I believe that although we are ordinary, we are capable of doing extraordinary things.

Keep your eyes on your future goals and make a commitment to yourself.

We can do this!

**LET'S GO!!!**

## **References**

Baron Zach, and Maxwell Robert. "The Life of (Virgil) Abloh." *GQ*, GQ, 1 Aug. 2016, www.gq.com/story/virgil-abloh-profile.

Gaines, Cork. "WHERE ARE THEY NOW? The 6 Quarterbacks Drafted before Tom Brady in the Infamous 2000 NFL Draft." *Business Insider*, Business Insider, 22 Jan. 2017, www.businessinsider.com/the-tom-brady-nfl-draft-quarterbacks-2017-1.

Nelson, Noelle, et al. "Emotions Know Best: The Advantage of Emotional versus Cognitive Responses to Failure." *Wiley Online Library*, Wiley/Blackwell, 8 Sept. 2017, onlinelibrary.wiley.com/doi/abs/10.1002/bdm.2042.

Rohn, Jim. "How to Bounce Back From Failure." *SUCCESS*, April 2016, www.success.com/rohn-how-to-bounce-back-from-failure/.

Zirm, Jordan. "How Stephen Curry Became the Best Shooter in the NBA." *STACK*, STACK, 4 June 2015, www.stack.com/a/stephen-curry-best-shooter.

# Bouncing Back from Failure

## *Additional Acknowledgements*

There is no way I could have written this without drawing inspiration from research and the people around me. I am grateful for the sources that I can cite from the Internet. Some of the stuff that I wrote about is from conversations that I've had with family and friends. I am thankful for everybody's input. I hope this book can help kids to work harder and be inspired. Thank you for reading.

# Bouncing Back from Failure

For additional inspiration, check out my 12 steps on how to turn your passion into progress in Kids Can Change the World!

**KIDS CAN CHANGE THE WORLD**

A MIDDLE SCHOOLER'S GUIDE FOR TURNING PASSION INTO PROGRESS

ADOM APPIAH

# Bouncing Back from Failure

PRAISE FOR
KIDS CAN CHANGE THE WORLD

"Powerful and very inspiring! Adom's tenacity for helping and encouraging others while overcoming obstacles is a testimony that transcends generations."
**- Hope Center for Children**

"A natural story teller with a message that transcends his generation."
**- Robert Tette, Winner - New York Association of Black Journalists Award for Personal Commentary**

"He is a young boy with a purpose. His warm demeanor is contagious..."
**-Mary Thomas, Chief Operating Officer - Spartanburg County Foundation**

"The book was very inspiring... I especially liked the mention of other kids' accomplishments."
**-6th Grader, New York**

"Adom uses simple concepts to show how anyone can live a life of significance, impacting their own communities."
**- Elsie Awadzi, 2nd Deputy Governor of the Bank of Ghana**

73

# Bouncing Back from Failure

Adom is the founder of Ball4Good, a nonprofit supporting communities through sports. He competed in the 2017 & 2018 Scripps National Spelling Bees.